Christ is Risen from the Dead

METROPOLITAN YOUSSEF

Edited and translated by
St. Mary and St. Moses Abbey

Contents

Christ is risen from the dead, rise with Him.... Christ is freed from the tomb, be freed from the bond of sin. The gates of hell are opened, and death is destroyed, and the old Adam is put aside, and the New is fulfilled; if any man be in Christ he is a new creature; be you renewed.

St. Gregory of Nazianzus

Oration XLV 1. (NPNF[2] 7)

1

Who Can Understand the Mystery of the Resurrection?

The subjects of the cross and the resurrection are among the most difficult subjects to understand with respect to unbelievers. As our teacher St. Paul the Apostle said in his first epistle to the Corinthians, "For the message of the cross is foolishness to those who are perishing, but to us who are being saved it is the power of God."[1] Then he says again, "But we preach Christ crucified, to the Jews a stumbling block and to the Greeks foolishness."[2] The unbeliever cannot understand the cross and the resurrection, and for that matter, cannot understand any of the Christian mysteries. Therefore, when an unbeliever starts attacking Christianity, he is excused, because the mystery of Christ cannot be understood by just anyone.

---

1   1 Corinthians 1:18.

2   1 Corinthians 1:23.

Types of People

St. Paul the Apostle, in his first epistle to the Corinthians, divided people into three groups.

The first group he called "the carnal man." This is the one who is led by the desires of the flesh. These are like infants, who are led by the desires of the flesh, meaning that their minds are not mature. The child wants to eat, to sleep, and so on. And so are the infants in Christ; they walk according to the desires of the flesh.

The second group he called "the natural man." These are the ones who may be mature, and their minds may be functional, but they do not have the Holy Spirit. Therefore, St. Paul the Apostle says, "Now we have received, not the spirit of the world, but the Spirit who is from God, that we might know the things that have been freely given to us by God."[3] I cannot understand the mystery of the resurrection, the mystery of Christ, through the spirit of the world, but I will understand by the Holy Spirit. He continues to say, "These things we also speak, not in words which man's wisdom teaches but which the Holy Spirit teaches, comparing spiritual things with spiritual."[4] Man's wisdom cannot explain the mystery of Christ. You cannot understand the spiritual things except by the Holy Spirit.

The person who does not have the Holy Spirit, however, St. Paul says about him, "But the natural man

------

3   1 Corinthians 2:12.
4   1 Corinthians 2:13.

does not receive the things of the Spirit of God, for they are foolishness to him; nor can he know them, because they are spiritually discerned."[5] Such a person would say, "Do you believe that God became Man? This is foolishness! Do you believe that God died on the cross? Does God die? What foolishness this is! Do you say that He rose from the dead? What foolishness you are in!" Therefore, you will not understand the mystery of Christ except by the Holy Spirit. How could an unbeliever, who has not received the Holy Spirit, understand the mystery of Christ?

Indeed, the Holy Spirit works with unbelievers, but from the outside. With respect to us, the believers, He dwells within us: "Do you not know that you are the temple of God and that the Spirit of God dwells in you?"[6] But the unbelievers who truly say, "Lord, guide me. Lord, enlighten my mind. I want to know where the truth is," with them the Holy Spirit works and guides them to the faith. This is the only way for the unbelievers. For them to understand, they must humble themselves and ask God to grant them the grace of understanding and enlightenment, so that they may understand the mystery of Christ.

As for the spiritual person, who has received the Holy Spirit, "He who is spiritual judges all things, yet he himself is rightly judged by no one."[7] By "judges all things," this means that the person understands the

---

5 1 Corinthians 2:14.

6 1 Corinthians 3:16.

7 1 Corinthians 2:15.

mystery of the resurrection on the level of faith, not on the level of the mind. And "he himself is rightly judged by no one" because "'who has known the mind of the Lord that he may instruct Him?' But we have the mind of Christ."[8]

Even the believers, who have received the Holy Spirit, if they practice Christianity with outward appearance only, then to them the mystery of Christ remains a difficult matter to understand, and so is the matter with the Holy Trinity, the mystery of the resurrection, and so on. The person must be filled with the Holy Spirit to understand the mystery of the resurrection.

The Resurrection is the Center of Christianity

The resurrection is the center of the preaching of the Apostles. Simply, as St. Paul the Apostle said, "And if Christ is not risen, then our preaching is empty and your faith is also empty."[9] If Christ's life had ended by His death and burial, then He would not have been God, but rather someone who had lived among us for a while, who had nice teachings; He would have been like all the prophets, who died and the story ended. Then we would not have been saved, but would have still been in our sins.

For this reason, Christianity is built upon the resurrection; and the resurrection is the center of

---

8   1 Corinthians 2:16.

9   1 Corinthians 15:14.

Christianity and the preaching of the Apostles. When we study the Book of Acts, we find that when St. Paul the Apostle spoke about God, the Jews accepted the teaching until he reached the resurrection, and then they turned against him; that is to say, they could not accept the idea of the resurrection. Even the Greeks or the Gentiles, when St. Paul preached to them in the Areopagus, listened to him very well until he spoke about the resurrection, and then they said, "'What does this babbler want to say?'... And when they heard of the resurrection of the dead, some mocked, while others said, 'We will hear you again on this matter.'"[10]

The unbelievers are stumbled by the subject of the resurrection and refuse to accept it, because the mystery of the resurrection is not revealed except through the Spirit of God, who is prepared to work in the unbelievers so that they may believe, and to work in the believers so that they may live the resurrection, because we must live the resurrection.

To Whom does God Reveal the Mystery of the Resurrection?

All these are mysteries: the mystery of the resurrection, of the Trinity, of the incarnation, and so on. These mysteries cannot be understood through studying and diligence, but rather through divine revelation. Take, for example, the mystery of the divinity of Christ. When Christ said to

---

10   Acts 17:18, 32.

them, "Who do men say that I, the Son of Man, am?"[11] according to human intellect, they said, "Some say John the Baptist, some Elijah, and others Jeremiah or one of the prophets."[12] "He said to them, 'But who do you say that I am?' Simon Peter answered and said, 'You are the Christ, the Son of the living God.'"[13] Then the Lord said to him, "Blessed are you, Simon Bar-Jonah, for flesh and blood has not revealed this to you, but My Father who is in heaven."[14] It is not a human revelation; this mystery needs to be revealed to us. God does not reveal it to just anyone. Even the resurrection, the Lord did not appear to all people, because these mysteries are revealed to a particular group of people. To whom does God reveal His mysteries?

1. God reveals Himself to those who fear His name. As the Scripture says, "The secret of the LORD is with those who fear Him."[15] Fear does not mean being scared of the Lord, but it means awe and respect for the holiness of God.

2. God reveals Himself to the humble. For example, St. Mary was the first one to know about the incarnation because of her humility: "For He has regarded the lowly state of His maidservant."[16]

---

11   Matthew 16:13.

12   Matthew 16:14.

13   Matthew 16:15–16.

14   Matthew 16:17.

15   Psalms 25:14.

16   Luke 1:48.

3. God reveals Himself to those who seek the truth faithfully, because God wants us to seek the truth in Him. For example, the story of St. Moses the Strong, when he asked the sun, "If you are God, tell me," and to the stars, "If you are God, tell me." He desired to know the truth until one day, a voice said to him, "Go to Scetis, and they will tell you."

4. God reveals Himself to those who do not rely on human wisdom. Some people want to understand God through human wisdom, but He will not be understood through it. And this is the problem of many atheists and unbelievers. Therefore, St. Paul the Apostle says, "For you see your calling, brethren, that not many wise according to the flesh, not many mighty, not many noble, are called."[17] He is saying to them that look at those who believed in Christ, that few of those were among the philosophers and wise men according to the flesh, few were among those who trusted in the strength of their personality, and few were among those who were proud of their positions and source of income.

As long as you trust in your strength, your knowledge, your wisdom, your position, and your money, then you will not be able to understand the mystery of the Lord. The mystery of the Lord is rather revealed to those who reject the wisdom of the world and who seek the wisdom of Christ. As St. Paul the Apostle said, "Has not God made foolish the wisdom of this world? For since, in the wisdom of God, the world through wisdom did not

---

17   1 Corinthians 1:26.

know God, it pleased God through the foolishness of the message preached to save those who believe."[18]

> *By your contempt of death: for in this we differ from the unbelievers. They may well fear death; since they have no hope of a resurrection. But you, who are travelling toward better things, and have the opportunity of meditating on the hope of the future; what excuse do you have, if while assured of a resurrection, you are yet at the same time as fearful of death, as those who believe not the resurrection?*

St. John Chrysostom

Homilies on the Statues V.6. (NPNF[1] 9)

---

18   1 Corinthians 1:20–21.

2

Participation in the Resurrection of Christ

1. Hearing the Word of God

The Lord spoke about two hours in the Gospel of St. John. The Lord said, "Most assuredly, I say to you, the hour is coming, and now is, when the dead will hear the voice of the Son of God; and those who hear will live."[19] Therefore, it is right now. Where is the resurrection here? When the dead hear the voice of the Son of God, they move from death—because they are dead—into life, that is, the resurrection.

In the same chapter, He spoke about the second hour. The first hour is now, and the second hour is in the future. He said, "Do not marvel at this; for the hour is coming in which all who are in the graves will hear His

---

19   John 5:25.

voice and come forth—those who have done good, to the resurrection of life, and those who have done evil, to the resurrection of condemnation."[20] Here, He did not call them "the dead" but "all who are in the graves." These will hear His voice in the last trumpet and will come forth.

In the first instance, he called them "the dead," that is, those who are dead spiritually. As He said in the Book of Revelation, "You have a name that you are alive, but you are dead,"[21] those who are ungodly or non-believers or living unrighteously. How will the resurrection happen in their lives? By hearing the voice of the Son of God; by listening to the word of God, they will hear His voice. He said, "now is"; the word "now" in the New Testament does not mean at the time of Christ, but it means every day in our lives. This means that we need to hear the voice of God every day in order to live the resurrection of Christ.

How can we hear the voice of God? The Lord said, "The words that I speak to you are spirit, and they are life."[22] The easiest way is by reading the Bible because the Bible is the word of God, through which God is speaking to you. The day on which you do not read the Bible, you do not hear the voice of God, and then you are abiding in spiritual death. The word of God is anointed by the Holy Spirit. It is not just a regular word; there is power in the word of God. We read that on the Day of Pentecost,

---

20   John 5:28–29.
21   Revelation 3:1.
22   John 6:63.

when Peter spoke, the listeners were pierced in their hearts. How were they pierced in their hearts? This is the power of the word of God; it is "sharper than any two-edged sword."[23] The word of God rebukes, the word of God convicts, the word of God corrects, the word of God teaches, and the word of God transforms the person. St. Augustine was living a very wicked life, but when he read some verses from Romans, these words transformed his life. And he converted completely from being a sinner to becoming a great saint in the Church. This is the power of the word of God. It has the power to convert you, to transform you, to change you.

2. Believing in Christ

In the story of the resurrection of Lazarus, the Lord Jesus Christ said to Martha, "I am the resurrection and the life. He who believes in Me, though he may die, he shall live."[24] Some people read the Bible so that they may attack and criticize the Bible; these will not move from death to life. But for a person to move from death to life, they need to believe in Christ. The main message of the Bible is to teach us about Christ, to make us believe in Christ, and without believing in Christ, there is no resurrection.

The Lord said to Martha, "He who believes in Me." Why is believing in Christ very important for the

---

23   Hebrews 4:12.
24   John 11:25.

resurrection? Because He is the only way; there is no other way to live. Believing in Him means clinging to Him, being united with Him, not just believing in a certain theory or a certain ideology; no, this is the faith of the demons. As St. James said, "You believe that there is one God. You do well. Even the demons believe—and tremble!"[25] But believing in Christ means that this faith can also transform and change your life. If I say, "I have been a believer in Christ for thirty, forty, fifty years," and my life is not transformed, then my faith is just a theoretical faith; it is an ideology. I accept this ideology, and that is it.

But the true faith is the faith that can convert you, transform you, and make you united with Christ, and your life is changed. We can see the transformation in St. Paul when he believed in Christ. He was a persecutor of the Church, but now he is persecuted for the Church of God—a great transformation. He was a murderer, in that he approved the death of St. Stephen, but now he died for Christ. Not only when he was martyred, but also as he said in the epistle to the Corinthians, "I die daily."[26] So you can see that this belief transformed the life of St. Paul completely from one extreme to another. This is the faith that will make us live the resurrection of Christ.

3. Living the Life of Repentance

In the parable of the prodigal son, the father said to the older brother, "It was right that we should make

---

25   James 2:19.

26   1 Corinthians 15:31.

merry and be glad, for your brother was dead and is alive again, and was lost and is found."[27] Why was he dead and is now alive? So, what happened in his life? That is what we call repentance. If we sin and are living in sin, we are under the sentence of death because "the wages of sin is death."[28] Christ bore our sins on the cross and died on the cross for our sins. So when we repent and believe in Christ, then the sentence of death is removed from us, and now we are alive; now we are risen with Christ. By repentance, we live the resurrection of Christ because every time we sin, we are under the sentence of death.

That is why repentance is a life. We practice it every day. We sin; yes, we are weak, "for no one is pure and without blemish, even though his life on earth be a single day."[29] As His Holiness Pope Shenouda used to say, "There is a sin of weakness and a sin of betrayal." The sin of Peter is a sin of weakness, but the sin of Judas was a sin of betrayal. There is a big difference between a person who sins because he is betraying Christ, like Judas, and a person who sins out of weakness. A person who is sinning out of weakness immediately repents like Peter. He wept bitterly, and he regretted what he did. That is why we need to examine ourselves daily and see what sins we committed this day, and offer sincere repentance to God so that we may hear God say about me, "He was dead and is alive again."

---

27   Luke 15:32.

28   Romans 6:23.

29   Litany for the Departed.

4. Baptism

St. Paul the Apostle says in his epistle to the Romans:

> How shall we who died to sin live any longer in it? Or do you not know that as many of us as were baptized into Christ Jesus were baptized into His death? Therefore we were buried with Him through baptism into death, that just as Christ was raised from the dead by the glory of the Father, even so we also should walk in newness of life. For if we have been united together in the likeness of His death, certainly we also shall be in the likeness of His resurrection, knowing this, that our old man was crucified with Him, that the body of sin might be done away with, that we should no longer be slaves of sin. For he who has died has been freed from sin.[30]

When Nicodemus met the Lord Jesus Christ, the Lord said to him, "That which is born of the flesh is flesh, and that which is born of the Spirit is spirit."[31] The biological birth from our parents is according to the law of the flesh, so we are born carnal. This is what He meant by "That which is born of the flesh is flesh." Carnal means under the influence of the flesh and the desires of the flesh. The first point is that we are born as carnal beings with Original Sin. The second point is that we

---

30   Romans 6:2–7.
31   John 3:6.

are born with a corrupted nature. The third point is that we are born with the potential to sin when we grow up because we have a corrupted nature.

How are we then born of the Spirit? This person who was born according to the flesh must die first and then must be born again; born again, however, not of flesh (because if he were born again of flesh, he would be carnal) but rather must be born again of the Spirit. And this is what happens in Baptism. The person who was born according to the flesh dies in the water of Baptism, and then he is raised and born again of the Spirit of God.

This is why the Lord said to Nicodemus, "Unless one is born of water and the Spirit, he cannot enter the kingdom of God."[32] In Baptism, I die with Christ, I am buried with Christ, and I also rise again;[33] I have participated in His death, and now I am participating in His resurrection. So I rise again with no sin, with no corruption, but although I might sin again out of weakness, these sins are forgiven and removed from me through repentance. That is why the fathers called repentance "the second baptism."

In Baptism, I am uniting with Christ; His righteousness will be considered my righteousness. Remember how the Lord Jesus Christ said to John the Baptist, "It is fitting for us to fulfill all righteousness."[34] No one, from Adam to the end of the ages, has been

---

32   John 3:5.

33   See Romans 6:4.

34   Matthew 3:15.

able to fulfill all the righteous requirements of the law, except Jesus Christ. So when I am united with Him, His righteousness becomes my own righteousness; as St. Paul said, "For as many of you as were baptized into Christ have put on Christ."[35] Therefore, without Baptism, I am not participating in the resurrection of Christ.

There is a beautiful tradition in the Coptic Church. When anyone is baptized, we do a procession for the baptized person usually at the end of the Divine Liturgy. During the Holy Fifty Days, we do not do it at the end of the Liturgy, but rather we do it with the procession of the resurrection. Through Baptism, this person is now risen with Christ. That is why we celebrate them while we are celebrating the resurrection of Christ.

5. Communion

Our Lord Jesus Christ said:

> Most assuredly, I say to you, unless you eat the flesh of the Son of Man and drink His blood, you have no life in you. Whoever eats My flesh and drinks My blood has eternal life, and I will raise him up at the last day. For My flesh is food indeed, and My blood is drink indeed. He who eats My flesh and drinks My blood abides in Me, and I in him. As the living Father sent Me, and I live because of the Father, so he who feeds on Me will live because of Me. This is the bread which

---

35   Galatians 3:27.

came down from heaven—not as your fathers ate the manna, and are dead. He who eats this bread will live forever.[36]

Communion is resurrection. The Body of Christ is not only a living Body, but is also a "life-giving Flesh";[37] It has the power to give me life. This is why when the Lord Jesus Christ touched the coffin of the son of the widow of Nain, the man rose from the dead, just by touching the coffin from the outside. When He called Lazarus, who had been dead for four days, Lazarus came out of the tomb. How much more is it when we are abiding in Him, and He in us?

To be united with Christ is necessary for our salvation because no one can fulfill the righteous requirements of the law except the Lord Jesus Christ. Therefore, I need to unite with Him, to be one with Him. Through this oneness, then I am righteous in Him. For example, if a poor girl marries a very rich man, through this oneness, through this bond, through this marriage, she becomes rich. So the richness of His righteousness becomes mine if I am united with Him, and this actual union happens in the Church Mysteries, particularly in Communion. That is why the Lord made it a condition: "Unless you eat the flesh of the Son of Man and drink His blood, you have no life in you."

As the body of Christ rose from the dead on the third day, when I am united with the Body of Christ, then I

---

36   John 6:53–58.

37   The Divine Liturgy – The Confession.

will have this power to be raised on the Second Coming of Christ. Also, no one with human nature was able to enter the heaven of heavens. That is why none of us were able to enter heaven, but in the incarnation, the Son of God took our humanity completely and then ascended with our humanity into the heaven of heavens. So He entered the heaven of heavens with our humanity. When we are united with Him, in Him we can enter the heaven of heavens, the place into which no human nature can enter. This means that if I want to enter by myself, I will be forbidden, but in Christ I have access to the heaven of heavens.

That is why He said, "I am the way, the truth, and the life,"[38] because He is the only way, the only true way to eternal life. But in order to be able to take Communion, you need to go through the previous steps; that is why you need to hear the word of God, believe, repent, be baptized, and then take Communion. If I am not living the life of repentance, then I will be guilty of the Body and Blood of the Lord Jesus Christ, as St. Paul said.[39] That is why I need to examine myself, repent, and confess my sins, so when I partake of His Body, it will not be a condemnation to me, but rather "salvation, remission of sins, and eternal life to those who partake of Him."[40]

---

38   John 14:6.
39   See 1 Corinthians 11:27.
40   The Divine Liturgy of St. Basil – The Confession.

6. Good Works

In his first epistle, St. John says, "We know that we have passed from death to life, because we love the brethren. He who does not love his brother abides in death. Whoever hates his brother is a murderer, and you know that no murderer has eternal life abiding in him."[41] He is basically saying that love is a resurrection: "We know that we have passed from death to life, because we love the brethren," passing from death to life is resurrection.

In the same epistle, he says that "we should love one another, not as Cain who was of the wicked one and murdered his brother."[42] Why did he kill his brother? Because he hated him. Murder is a result of hatred. And the Bible teaches us in Genesis that he who kills should be killed.[43] Therefore, he who kills is under the sentence of death, unless he repents, of course. If I hate someone, then I am a murderer even if I do not literally kill him, but because hatred leads to murder, then I am a murderer. And a murderer is under the penalty of death.

Therefore, when I move from hatred to love, then I am passing from death to life. St. John in the same epistle said, "Let us not love in word or in tongue, but in deed and in truth."[44] We should love in action, by works. I cannot say that I love you with words, and my heart is full of hatred, but love should be demonstrated in action; this is true love.

---

41   1 John 3:14–15.
42   1 John 3:11–12.
43   See Genesis 9:6.
44   1 John 3:18.

We participate in the resurrection by charitable deeds, by loving one another, by forgiving one another, by reconciling with one another, by loving even our enemies: "Love your enemies, bless those who curse you, do good to those who hate you, and pray for those who spitefully use you and persecute you."[45] That is love; that is the resurrection.

And having made his proclamation to the spirits in hell, who had once disobeyed, he ascended victorious, having raised up his own temple as a kind of first-fruits of our hope, made resurrection from the dead a way on which revived nature can travel.[46]

St. Cyril of Alexandria

---

45   Matthew 5:44.

46   St. Cyril of Alexandria, *Festal Letters 1–12*, Amidon P.R., trans. (Washington, D.C.: The Catholic University of America Press, 2009), 84.

3

Sound Faith as a Requirement to Enjoy the Resurrection

Jesus, our God, came and took our human nature, uniting human nature with His divinity. One of the reasons for the incarnation was to defeat death in human nature, to abolish death as a human being, and then He would give us this power. When we are one with Him, we can defeat the power of death and the power of the grave. And in this way, He is the resurrection of us all, as we say in the Litany for the Gospel. He is our resurrection because all of us were under the sentence of death. Therefore, He came to give us life; resurrection means moving from death to life. As we read in the Gospel of St. John, "I have come that they may have life, and that they may have it more abundantly."[47]

---

47   John 10:10.

Therefore, during the journey of the Holy Fifty days after the resurrection, the Church takes us step by step. The first step is faith, to believe in Him, because if we do not believe in Jesus Christ, how will His resurrection be our resurrection? As it is written in the gospel of St. John, "And truly Jesus did many other signs in the presence of His disciples, which are not written in this book; but these are written that you may believe that Jesus is the Christ, the Son of God, and that believing you may have life in His name."[48] Then, when you believe that Jesus is the Messiah, you will have eternal life. Faith is not everything, but, as I said, it is a journey. One of the things we need in order for His resurrection to become our resurrection is faith.

And the Church gives us the example of Thomas. Thomas was one of the disciples and heard the teaching of our Lord Jesus Christ. And he was one of the twelve whom the Lord sent and told them, "Heal the sick, cleanse the lepers, raise the dead, cast out demons."[49] So he performed miracles in the name of Jesus. But on the day of the resurrection, when the Lord appeared to the disciples, Thomas was not with them. When he returned and was told that Jesus had appeared to the disciples, and that they had seen him, Thomas doubted. Despite all the teaching and all the miracles that Thomas was an eyewitness to, he doubted the resurrection of Christ and said, "Unless I see in His hands the print of the nails, and put my finger into the print of the nails, and put my

---

48   John 20:30–31.
49   Matthew 10:8.

hand into His side, I will not believe."[50] He asked not only to see Him, but to put his finger in the print of the nails, because He can be just a spirit.

Then, to confirm his faith, the Lord appeared to him on the eighth day. Why the eighth day? The Lord waited to confirm that Sunday is the day of the resurrection. We celebrate the resurrection of Christ on Sunday by celebrating the Eucharist, and to replace the Sabbath of the old covenant with the new Sabbath, that is Sunday, the day of the Lord, because the word Sabbath means rest, so our new Sabbath, our rest now, is in the resurrection of the Lord. That is why He did not appear on the second day or the third day, but He appeared after one week on Sunday also. And the Church celebrates Thomas Sunday as one of the minor feasts of the Lord because He confirmed His resurrection to the eleven.

The Lord said to Thomas, "Reach your finger here, and look at My hands; and reach your hand here, and put it into My side. Do not be unbelieving, but believing."[51] This was important because the disciples would preach the resurrection to the whole world. What if one of them is doubting the resurrection of the Lord? But He told him, "Blessed are those who have not seen and yet have believed."[52] And I think this generation in particular needs to understand this word, because the current generation exalts seeing more than believing; and they say, "If we do

---

50   John 20:25.
51   John 20:27.
52   John 20:29.

not see, we will not believe; if you cannot prove it to me scientifically, I will not believe." And that is why atheism is now spreading because they want to apply the scientific method to the principles of faith, but the Lord is teaching us that those who believe without seeing are blessed.

Thomas was one of the disciples, and we cannot call him a nonbeliever; he was a believer. So not every type of faith will give us eternal life.

Types of Faith

As we have said, faith is required to enjoy the resurrection of Christ, for His resurrection to be our resurrection. All of us might say, "Thank God we are believers and are in the Church," but we will talk about the different types of faith, for not all these types of faith can get us into the kingdom of heaven.

1. The Thomas Faith

The Thomas faith is based on seeing, on the scientific method. "Unless I see in His hands the print of the nails, and put my finger into the print of the nails, and put my hand into His side, I will not believe."[53] This faith is not the Christian faith; this faith is not the faith that actually makes the resurrection of Christ our resurrection. Therefore, "Blessed are those who have not seen and yet have believed."[54]

---

53   John 20:25.

54   John 20:29.

2. The Mary and Martha Faith

Again, we cannot call Mary and Martha nonbelievers, for they were believers. But let us examine their faith. Both of them said to the Lord Jesus Christ, "Lord, if You had been here, my brother would not have died."[55] So they believe that Jesus Christ has power over sickness, and He could have healed Lazarus. But since Lazarus is now dead, it is over; You cannot do anything. It is as if they were telling Him, "You do not have power over death; yes, You have power over illness, You could have healed Him, but now he has been in the tomb for four days. There is a stench."

That is why the Lord repeated several times, saying to them, "Did I not say to you that if you would believe you would see the glory of God?"[56] It is as if the Lord were saying, "Your faith is deficient and is not complete because you believe that the Lord can do certain things but cannot do other things." Sometimes we have the same faith. If there is a big problem, we actually doubt that God will do anything about it. But we need to have perfect faith.

3. The Faith of the Demons

St. James spoke about the faith of the demons, saying, "You believe that there is one God. You do well. Even the demons believe—and tremble!"[57] The demons

---

55   John 11:21.

56   John 11:40.

57   James 2:19.

believe in the existence of God and confessed that Jesus is the Christ, the Son of God, when He healed Peter's mother-in-law and then healed many people who were sick and also people who were demon-possessed. This is the gospel we pray in the eleventh hour of the Agpeya. The demons said, "You are the Christ, the Son of God!"[58] Although the demons believe, this belief is not translated into action, to live according to this faith. The demons believe that Jesus is the Christ, the Son of the living God, but their faith is not validated by works.

That is why St. James said, "Faith without works is dead."[59] Not only works, but faith also, without love, has no value. St. Paul said, "Though I have all faith, so that I could remove mountains, but have not love, I am nothing,"[60] love that is expressed toward God and toward others, love that is sacrificial, unconditional, limitless; this is the love that God expects from us.

4. The True Faith in the Resurrected Lord Jesus Christ

Everyone in the world has a belief system. Even atheists believe in the non-existence of God. So, any belief system—any dogma—other than that Jesus is Christ, the Son of the living God who rose from the dead for our salvation, any other faith is destructive. I am saying it will destroy the person eternally, that there is no salvation for

---

58   Luke 4:41.
59   James 2:26.
60   1 Corinthians 13:2.

such a person. As we read in the Gospel of St. John, "He who believes in the Son has everlasting life; and he who does not believe the Son shall not see life, but the wrath of God abides on him."[61]

Growing Your Faith by Taking Risks of Faith

Fatih will never grow unless you take the risk of faith. What do I mean by "taking the risk of faith"? Some commandments in the Bible look risky from the outside, but unless you take this risk and keep these commandments, you will never grow in the faith, since by taking the risk, you will see how God will deal with you and how God is faithful in His promises. For example, let us examine a story from the Scripture: the widow of Zarephath of Sidon. Elijah went to her and told her, "Make me a small cake from it first."[62] She told him that all that she had was a bit of flour and a small amount of oil, and that was it. But she actually took the risk of faith; she believed him. He is the man of God, and she made a cake for him first. Because of this, God blessed her, and the flour and oil did not run out until the famine was over.

Therefore, by obeying the commandment of God, her faith grew, because her faith now is not what she heard about God, but what she experienced herself. There are commandments like giving, helping others, forgiving, and reconciliation. All these commandments come at a risk. How can I give while I am in need? How can I reconcile

---

61   John 3:36.

62   1 Kings 17:13.

while this person hurt me? How can I forgive while this person does not love me? In all these commandments, we follow our logic, not following the commandment of God, which means we lack faith, because if we believe without seeing, we will apply these commandments in our lives. But we are reluctant to take the risk of faith, to apply these commandments in our lives.

St. Paul, in his epistle to the Hebrews, explained something very important. He said to us that Abraham, when he went to offer his son Isaac, believed that God would give him Isaac back. And St. Paul explained how Abraham said that if God was able to create Isaac from the dead womb of Sarah and from his deadness as an old man, then even if he offered Isaac as a sacrifice, God would raise him from the dead.[63] That is why he went without any reluctance to offer Isaac as a sacrifice, and as he believed, God gave him Isaac back, and he returned to his home with Isaac.

We need to be willing to take the risk of faith. If we want our faith to grow, but we are following our logic, and we only keep the commandments of God when they make sense to us, then our faith will never grow. In the first commission, the Lord sent His disciples and told them, "Take nothing for the journey, neither staffs nor bag nor bread nor money; and do not have two tunics apiece."[64] And when they returned, He asked them a question, "'When I sent you without money bag, knapsack, and sandals, did

---

63   See Hebrews 11:17.

64   Luke 9:3.

you lack anything?' So they said, 'Nothing,'"[65] because they trusted God. They had faith in Him. When He told them, "Take nothing with you," He would provide.

We see someone like St. Anthony the Great. He sold everything and went to live in the desert, not worrying about how he could provide for himself. But God provided for him, and He took care of him. The same happened for St. Paul the First Hermit, and the same for everyone who took the risk of faith. If you want your faith to grow, you need to obey the commandments of God without questioning. If God said so, then my part is to obey Him. And when I obey God without questioning Him, my faith will grow.

"And truly Jesus did many other signs in the presence of His disciples, which are not written in this book; but these are written that you may believe that Jesus is the Christ, the Son of God, and that believing you may have life in His name."[66]

Thomas, who thrust his hand into His side, and his fingers into the prints of the nails. For it was for our sakes that he so carefully handled Him; and what you, who were not there present, would have sought, he being present, by God's Providence, did seek.

St. Cyril of Jerusalem

The Catechetical Lectures XIII.39. (NPNF[2] 7)

---

65   Luke 22:35.
66   John 20:30–31.

4

The Journey from Resurrection to Resurrection through Holy Week

We need to compare the resurrection of Lazarus with the resurrection of our Lord Jesus Christ. When Lazarus came out of the tomb, he came out clothed and wrapped in the graveclothes. Even the handkerchief was still on his face, and the Lord told them, "Loose him, and let him go."[67] But when the Lord Jesus Christ rose from the dead, He rose from the dead while the graveclothes were left in the tomb. He did not come out with the graveclothes. And when Peter and John went to the tomb, they saw the graveclothes placed there carefully, and the handkerchief that had been on the face of the Lord was folded and placed alone in a different place.

What is the significance of this? Lazarus rose with a mortal body, the same body. The nature of his body did

---

67   John 11:44.

not change. That is why he died again. He lived for many years and then died. But the Lord Jesus Christ, when He rose from the dead, rose with a glorified body, the body with which all of us will be raised, in the Second Coming. This is why St. Paul said about the Lord Jesus Christ, "Now Christ is risen from the dead, and has become the firstfruits of those who have fallen asleep,"[68] although we know that Lazarus was raised before the Lord Jesus Christ, and also the son of the widow of Nain and the daughter of Jairus.

Jesus was called the firstfruits of those who rose from the dead because He is the first one who rose from the dead with the glorified body, the body of the resurrection. And St. Paul said that as Jesus rose from the dead with the glorified body, all of us will be raised with the same glorified body.[69] He even told us, "Behold, I tell you a mystery: We shall not all sleep, but we shall all be changed—in a moment, in the twinkling of an eye, at the last trumpet."[70] Meaning what? If the Lord Jesus Christ returns now—that is, the Second Coming—and we are still alive, then in a twinkling of an eye, in a moment, we will be changed into the glorified body.

Also, we read in the Book of Revelation, "Blessed and holy is he who has part in the first resurrection. Over such the second death has no power."[71] What does this mean? What is the first resurrection, and what is the second death?

---

68   1 Corinthians 15:20.

69   See Philippians 3:21.

70   1 Corinthians 15:51–52.

71   Revelation 20:6.

And if we are speaking about the first resurrection, then there is a first death, and if we are speaking about the second resurrection, then there is a second death. The first death is the death of sin. As the Lord said to one of the angels in the Book of Revelation, "You have a name that you are alive, but you are dead."[72] And as we read in the Gospel of St. John, "The hour is coming, and now is, when the dead will hear the voice of the Son of God; and those who hear will live."[73] So the first death is the death of sin, and the first resurrection is the resurrection of repentance. The second death is the eternal death, and the second resurrection is the resurrection when the Lord Jesus Christ comes. Those will be raised with the glorified body and inherit the kingdom of God. That is why the Book of Revelation says, "Blessed and holy is he who has part in the first resurrection, [who lived the life of repentance]. Over such the second death, [the eternal damnation], has no power."

Resurrection from Sin to the Resurrection of Eternal Life in a Week

Saturday

The resurrection of Lazarus represents our first resurrection, which is the resurrection from the death of sin. The resurrection of Christ is our second resurrection.

---

72   Revelation 3:1.
73   John 5:25.

Therefore, the Church, from Lazarus Saturday, is preparing us for the Feast of the Resurrection, telling us that we need to be raised with Lazarus from the death of sin. If we are abiding in sin, then we are dead, although we may be physically alive. As the Lord said, "You have a name that you are alive, but you are dead."[74] That is, the death of sin. In order to participate in the first resurrection, we need repentance, Confession, Baptism, Chrismation, and Communion. All these Mysteries are essential for our participation in the resurrection of repentance.

Sunday

Also, we need to live a godly life and to let Christ reign in our hearts. This is why on Hosanna Sunday the people received the Lord Jesus Christ as their King: "Hosanna! 'Blessed is He who comes in the name of the LORD!' The King of Israel!"[75] In their mind, He was an earthly King. He came to restore the kingdom of David. But we, the believers, know better. We know that Jesus said, "My kingdom is not of this world."[76] He is a heavenly King who reigns in our hearts.

So the journey starts from the Lazarus Saturday by repenting and dedicating our hearts to God. Then we need to let the Lord Jesus Christ reign in our hearts, in our minds, in our thoughts, in every single area of our

---

74 Revelation 3:1.

75 John 12:13.

76 John 18:36.

lives. Nothing is excluded. To reign over my life means I do everything for Him and by Him, to do everything according to His law and for His glory. This is the meaning of letting Him reign over my life.

Once the Lord enters our lives, we who are struggling with sin and temptation, God will cleanse us from both. In like manner, when He entered Jerusalem, the first thing He did was that He went into the temple and cleansed it. He cleansed the temple twice. The first time was mentioned in the second chapter of the Gospel of St. John, at the beginning of His ministry, and the second time on the day after Hosanna Sunday, after He entered Jerusalem. So we need to allow the Lord to enter our heart and reign over it, so that He may cleanse our heart from all the filthiness of this world and give us a pure heart for Him.

Monday

Some people will allow Christ to reign over them, but in a hypocritical way, not sincerely. They might say, "Yes, Christ is my King. I'm a believer." And they may do some practices; they may pray, go to church, take Communion. But as the Lord said, "This people honors Me with their lips, but their heart is far from Me."[77] That is why, with the cleansing of the temple, another incident happened: cursing the fig tree.

The fig tree represents the hypocrites, because when the Lord saw the fig tree, He found many leaves, but there

---

77   Mark 7:6.

was no fruit. It is the life of a hypocrite, who has many leaves, many activities, but these activities are external. There is no fruit in his heart. He did not bear the fruit of the Holy Spirit in his heart. We need to let the Lord reign in our hearts sincerely, genuinely, not like the hypocrites, but in a faithful way. And when the Lord enters my heart and reigns over me, He will teach me. He will enlighten my mind.

Tuesday

Christ spent the whole of Tuesday in the temple, teaching and answering the questions of the people. Some people benefited from His teaching; others did not. Yet others came just to test Him, and when He spoke about them, they started to make a conspiracy about how they might kill Him and get rid of Him.

God gives us the Bible, His word, to teach us, to enlighten us. Where is the Bible in my life? Where is the place of the word of God in my life? Do I know the word of God? How can we say that the Lord reigns in us and that we are living the life of repentance, while we are in total estrangement from the word of God? Not only does the word of God make us intellectually know the commandments of God, but the word of God is a living word, piercing into my heart, transforming me, changing me. As St. Paul said in the epistle to the Hebrews, "For the word of God is living and powerful, and sharper than any two-edged sword."[78] The process of

---

78   Hebrews 4:12.

cleansing is through the word of God. As the Lord said to His disciples, "You are already clean because of the word which I have spoken to you."[79]

Wednesday

Then on Wednesday, the Church makes a comparison between two persons. One person is Judas Iscariot, who was one of the twelve, who received the gifts of the Holy Spirit, who performed many miracles, who cast out demons, but he did not allow God to reign completely over his heart. As we have said earlier, nothing is excluded. But Judas kept back part of his heart, not being under the reign of Christ: a part that loved money. That is why he betrayed the Lord Jesus Christ and delivered Him for thirty pieces of silver.

On the other side, we have this sinful woman who brought an alabaster flask of a very costly, fragrant oil. Its value was three hundred denarii, and one denarius was a worker's wages per day. To understand the value of three hundred denarii today, if the wages of a worker today is roughly fifty dollars, then three hundred denarii mean fifteen thousand dollars. So she brought this fragrant oil that cost fifteen thousand dollars, and she poured it on the head of the Lord Jesus Christ as an expression of her love, an expression of her repentance, an expression that the Lord reigned over her heart completely; nothing was excluded.

---

79   John 15:3.

Here we have one of the disciples betraying the Lord for a few dollars—thirty pieces of silver—just a few dollars, less than a hundred dollars. And we have this lady who let the Lord reign over her heart and poured this very costly oil because she loved much.

Thursday

Our journey has now reached Covenant Thursday, on which the Lord washed the feet of the disciples. He came to wash our sins, because in our spiritual journey, our spiritual feet get dirty. So washing the feet here symbolizes the washing of our sins. So the Lord understands that we, as weak human beings, may fall, but every time we fall, we need to rise again and to live the life of repentance. And He is willing to wash my feet, willing to wash my sins and purify me. Every time I come to the Lord confessing my sins, asking His forgiveness, He will forgive me.

Not only does the Lord want me to be pure and clean, but He also wants to be united with me. That is why on Thursday, He gave us His Body and His Blood. "'Take, eat; this is My body'…. 'Drink from it, all of you. For this is My blood'"[80] The ultimate goal for many of us may be that we be saved. To be saved means to go to heaven and to escape the lake of fire. This may be the ultimate goal for many of us, but for God, the ultimate goal is not only our salvation, but our union with Him, to be one with Him. That is why He described Himself as the groom, and we are the bride, and the two shall become one.

---

80   Matthew 26:26–28.

Friday

If I am one with Him, to be glorified with Him, I need to suffer with Him and to carry my cross. As the Lord said, "If anyone desires to come after Me, let him deny himself, and take up his cross daily, and follow Me."[81] This brings us to Friday: carrying the cross in this world. We are not of this world, and the world is becoming more evil every day. And we feel that we have no place here in the world. We are persecuted in this world. We cannot defend the biblical values and the biblical morals. Everything became against Christ, against the Bible, against Christianity.

But this does not bother us. It is a cross that we carry here to be glorified with Him. Even if the world did not accept us, even if the world did not love us, we should know that they did the same to the Lord Jesus Christ. They crucified Him after all the goodness that He did to each one of them. And we need to say with St. Paul, "I have been crucified with Christ,"[82] "by whom the world has been crucified to me, and I to the world."[83] The world cannot tempt me, because the world is crucified to me, and I am crucified to the world. This means that I do not desire anything from the world. I die to the world, as the Lord died on the cross. "It is no longer I who live, but Christ lives in me."[84] We are considered dead to the world, but we are alive in spirit to God.

---

81   Luke 9:23.
82   Galatians 2:20.
83   Galatians 6:14.
84   Galatians 2:20.

We started this journey, the journey that started by the life of repentance, the resurrection of Lazarus; letting the Lord reign over our heart on Hosanna Sunday; letting the Lord cleanse our heart, the purification of the temple; not living a hypocritical life like the fig tree, but bearing the fruit of the Spirit in our heart; listening to the word of God, which purifies and cleanses us; not doing like Judas, who kept part of his heart for the love of money. But we should do like the lady, who gave all her love and all her life, when she poured this very costly ointment on the head of the Lord.

Christ understands my weakness. So every time I sin, He comes and washes my feet, washing my sins and granting me forgiveness of my sins. And as I said, He wants to commune with me, to be one with me, to unite me to Himself, so we will become one. In this oneness, I am crucified with Him. I suffer with Him to be glorified with Him. In this oneness, I die to the world, because I am not of this world. Our citizenship is in heaven. We are strangers here.

The person who starts this journey and completes it, then in the Second Coming of Christ, will enjoy the second resurrection, resurrection with the glorified body, reigning in the kingdom of heaven forever with the Lord Jesus Christ. This is our journey. That is why I said that there are two resurrections, and Holy Week is in between the two resurrections, which explains our journey in this world. Therefore, let us start this step by step with the Lord Jesus Christ. So when we celebrate the Feast of the Resurrection and say, "Christ is risen. Truly, He is risen," this will be our resurrection. As we say in the Litany for the Gospel, "For You are the resurrection of us all."

I confess the Cross, because I know of the Resurrection; for if, after being crucified, He had remained as He was, I had not perhaps confessed it, for I might have concealed both it and my Master; but now that the Resurrection has followed the Cross, I am not ashamed to declare it.

St. Cyril of Jerusalem

The Catechetical Lectures XIII.4. (NPNF[2] 7)

5

Enactment of the Resurrection

One of the main features of the Divine Liturgy of the Feast of the Resurrection is the enactment of the resurrection, in which two deacons stand outside the altar, while the priest—or the highest-ranking clergyman in attendance—stands inside the altar. Then a dialogue starts between the two deacons outside and the highest-ranking clergyman, whether the Patriarch, a bishop, or a priest.

The deacons say, "Christ is risen," and then from inside, the high priest replies, "Truly He is risen." Then the deacons quote verses from Psalm twenty-four,[85] and say, "Lift up your gates, O rulers! And be raised up, O eternal gates, that the King of glory may enter." Then the high priest replies from inside, "Who is this King of glory?" Then they reply, "The Lord, the powerful, the strong, the mighty, victorious in battles; He is the King

---

85   Psalm twenty-three according to the Septuagint.

of glory." Then he opens the veil, and the procession of the resurrection starts. Do we understand this enactment and its meaning? What are the eternal gates?

Explanation of the Enactment of the Resurrection

Our Lord Jesus Christ descended into Hades to bring all the souls that were taken captive, to take them into the Paradise of joy. If we go back to Genesis, after the fall of Adam and Eve, the tree of life was guarded by an angel, and then the doors of Paradise were closed from that time forward.

What is the tree of life? The tree of life is the bread of life that came down from heaven. On the altar, we have the Body and Blood of our Lord Jesus Christ. This is the tree of life. And the high priest inside the altar represents the angel who is guarding the tree of life, guarding the bread of life. And these doors are the doors of Paradise, which are closed.

Our Lord Jesus Christ in His ministry on earth was always surrounded by angels, as we read in the Gospel of St. Matthew, "Angels came and ministered to Him."[86] I would like you to imagine the Lord Jesus Christ coming from Hades, having with Him the souls of Adam, Eve, and all the patriarchs, all the prophets, all the saints of the Old Testament, and also with the angels. So the dialogue is between the angels that were serving the Lord

---

86 Matthew 4:11.

Jesus Christ and the angel that was guarding the bread of life, the tree of life inside.

They are sharing the good news, the greeting: Christ is risen; truly He is risen. Then the angel says joyfully, "Lift up your gates, O rulers! And be raised up, O eternal gates." Now these doors will be opened and will never be closed again. It is a symbol of the reconciliation between God and mankind.

Then, when the angel from inside says, "Who is this King of glory?" not because he does not know Him, but this question is said so that the whole world may know who the King of glory is. The angels respond, "The Lord, the powerful, the strong, the mighty, victorious in battles; He is the King of glory." You saw Him on Friday on the cross, being weak. No, He is strong and mighty, the Lord who is victorious in battles.

Then the gates are opened, the lights are turned on, and the procession starts. Therefore, the icon of the resurrection during the enactment should be outside, not inside, because the icon represents Jesus Christ, and the deacons should be outside. Then, when the veil is opened, the deacons with the icon enter into Paradise, symbolizing the entry of our Lord Jesus Christ with all the souls. Then they make a procession three times around the altar, and then three times around the nave of the church.

Why do they go outside the sanctuary? As we read in the Gospel of St. Matthew, during the time of the resurrection, many of the souls of the departed were raised and appeared to people in Jerusalem. It says, "The graves were opened; and many bodies of the saints who had fallen asleep were raised; and coming out of the graves after His resurrection, they went into the holy city and appeared to many,"[87] and they told them, "Christ is risen! Christ is risen!" These saints who rose from the dead at this moment were preaching the resurrection of Christ to many in Jerusalem. When the procession goes outside the altar, it represents the resurrection of many of the bodies of the saints who had fallen asleep, and coming out of the graves after His resurrection, they went into the holy city and appeared to many.

That is why during the procession of the resurrection, we chant, "Christ is risen."[88] They were preaching, "Christ is risen from the dead, trampling down death by death and upon those in the tombs [like us] bestowing life." We were in the tombs, but now are risen, and we are granted eternal life.

Then what happened to these saints? They died again and returned to their graves. When they died, they rested back in Paradise. That is why the procession ends in the altar. So we go in the altar, and we do the final procession, representing that these souls that were risen are now reposed in the Paradise of joy, waiting for the general resurrection at the Second Coming of the Lord Jesus Christ.

After we do one procession in the altar, the icon of Christ, which entered the altar for the second time, represents that after He had appeared for forty days,

---

87   Matthew 27:52–53.

88   Cop. Ⲭⲣⲓⲥⲧⲟⲥ ⲁ̀ⲛⲉⲥⲧⲏ.

He then ascended to the heavens. That is why, after the procession, the icon of the resurrection that is used in the procession should be inside the altar, not outside. And this is why we do the procession for forty days, because during these forty days the Lord appeared to many people. One time, He appeared to 500 persons together as St. Paul said in his first epistle to the Corinthians.[89] Between the Ascension and Pentecost, there are many views about this, but the traditional view in the Coptic Church is that there is no procession after Ascension Thursday, except on the sixth Sunday, because Sunday is the day of the resurrection and on the Sunday of Pentecost. So only two processions are performed after the Ascension, and it is a whole procession.

Why is the Great Event of Opening the Paradise not Celebrated?

The Church wanted to celebrate this day, but the opening of Paradise was on Good Friday, so we cannot leave the celebration of Good Friday to celebrate the opening of Paradise. Also, on Bright Saturday, the Lord is in the tomb, so we cannot leave the celebration of Bright Saturday to celebrate the opening of Paradise. Then after this is Sunday which is the Feast of the Resurrection.

However, the first day after the very important days of Good Friday, Bright Saturday, and the Resurrection Sunday is Monday, so the Church made this day a

---

89   See 1 Corinthians 15:6.

celebration of the opening of Paradise and restoring Adam and all his children to the Paradise of joy.

Here is the evidence. There is a certain Psali for the resurrection on Monday, which is about Adam and the restoration to the Paradise of joy. So we do not pray the usual Adam Psali on this Monday, but there is a special Psali for this Monday. And this day is called *Sham al-Nasim*, which is not an Arabic word. Resurrection Monday is the day on which the people celebrate the return to the Paradise of joy. That is why people go to the gardens or parks and spend the day there, to remind us of the return to the Paradise of joy. This is a representation of the Garden of Eden. It is not a celebration of the spring season, but rather of the opening of the Paradise of joy.

In the Litany for the Seeds and the Herbs, the Coptic text says, "*niciti nem nicim.*" *Niciti* means plants, and *nicim* means the green herbs. Therefore, the Coptic phrase *chom en-nicim*[90] does not mean smelling the beautiful weather but literally means the green pasture. The Church called this day the day of the green pasture because we are celebrating the return of Adam, Eve, and their children to the Paradise of joy. It is a Christian feast.

---

90   Cop. Ϭⲱⲙ ⲛ̀ⲛⲓⲥⲓⲙ.

6

Blessings of the Resurrection

1. Human Nature Defeated Death

Our Lord Jesus Christ is God, who in the fullness of time took flesh, meaning that He took our humanity, our human nature. Because our human nature was corrupted after the fall of Adam and Eve, and was under the sentence of death, sin abode in our nature. So the Lord took our nature to heal it, to renew it. When we say that our Lord Jesus Christ rose from the dead, we are celebrating the resurrection of human nature that the Lord Jesus Christ, the Son of God, took, making it His body, His humanity. So we are celebrating how this human nature defeated death. That is why in the Litany for the Gospel, we say, "For You are the resurrection of us all." Now death no longer has authority over our human nature, because Jesus rose from the dead, meaning all of us will be raised from the dead if we are united with Him, if we are abiding in Him. Therefore, we are not just happy because Jesus, whom we love, rose from the dead, but rather because our human nature defeated death.

2. Human Nature Can Defeat Sin

The Lord bore our sins, bore our curse, and died on the cross. By His death on the cross, He paid the wages of sin, which is death.[91] Then He rose from the dead. This resurrection means our human nature can defeat sin. We can overcome sin. Sin no longer has authority over us. To further explain it, think about a deadly disease. When a person is attacked by a deadly disease, like cancer, for example, we expect this person to die. But if they discovered a medicine that could cure this disease completely, then we would not be worried about this disease anymore, because there is a treatment.

In the same way, sin was a deadly spiritual disease. Why deadly? "For the wages of sin is death."[92] But the Lord Jesus Christ defeated the power of sin by His resurrection. So with repentance, sin is not deadly anymore. That is why St. Paul mentioned in his first epistle to the Corinthians, in the chapter of the resurrection, when he spoke about the resurrection of Christ, "O Death, where is your sting? O Hades, where is your victory? The sting of death is sin."[93] So if sin pierces me like a sting, I will die. But now, with the resurrection of Christ, sin lost its power. That is why he continues, saying, "But thanks be

---

91   Romans 6:23.

92   Romans 6:23.

93   1 Corinthians 15:55–56.

to God, who gives us the victory through our Lord Jesus Christ."[94] Through the resurrection, sin is no longer a deadly spiritual disease. With repentance, I can be healed.

3. Human Nature was Delivered from Corruption

Through Adam's sin, our nature became corrupted, although God created us in incorruption, as we pray in the Prayer of Reconciliation in the Liturgy of St. Basil, "O God, the Great, the Eternal, who formed man in incorruption." However, through the cross and death and the resurrection, we now became a new creation in the Lord Jesus Christ. So our nature is renewed through the resurrection of Christ. We are no longer corrupted.

And this was very important to prepare for another important step. Jesus came as our bridegroom, and we are His bride. It was impossible for God, who is holy, to be united with us while we are corrupted. There is no fellowship between light and darkness,[95] no fellowship between corruption and incorruption. That is why our nature must be renewed before this union can take place between Christ and us. So through the resurrection of Christ, the union between God and us became possible, and we became a dwelling place for the Holy Spirit: "Your body is the temple of the Holy Spirit who is in you."[96]

Our Lord Jesus Christ said to Mary Magdalene, "But go to My brethren and say to them, 'I am ascending to My

---

94   1 Corinthians 15:57.
95   See 2 Corinthians 6:14.
96   1 Corinthians 6:19.

Father and your Father, and to My God and your God.'"[97] How has His Father become our Father, and how has His God become our God? Because of this union between our Lord Jesus Christ and us, which only became possible after the resurrection of Christ. The Father is the Father to the Son by nature and has only one begotten Son. But by the resurrection and this union between the Son and us, His Father became our Father by adoption. And because Christ became like us in everything through the incarnation, God, who is our God, He called Him His God also. As we call the Father, "God" by nature, Jesus calls the Father "God" also because He and we became one.

4. Access to the Heaven of Heavens

Christ said, "I am ascending." He ascended with our human nature. In the fraction of Bright Saturday, there is emphasis on how we entered with our nature into the heavens, the place where no human nature can enter. We pray in the fraction and say:

> You are the King of the ages, the Immortal, the Everlasting, the Logos of God who is above all, the Shepherd of the rational sheep, the High Priest of the good things to come, who ascended into the heavens and has become higher than the heavens. He went within the veil to the Holy place of the Holies, the place into which anyone of human nature cannot enter.

---

97   John 20:17.

Human nature cannot enter the heaven of heavens, but now Jesus entered the heaven of heavens with our humanity. And since he entered with our human nature, He has given us access also to enter the heaven of heavens, which was impossible without the resurrection.

5. A New Nature

In Baptism, we are buried with the Lord Jesus Christ and are raised with Him. The old nature dies in the water of Baptism. And when we rise with Him in Baptism, we have a new nature, a nature that is pure and clean, a nature that has the righteousness of Christ. That is why this nature can be united with God, as St. Paul said, "For as many of you as were baptized into Christ have put on Christ."[98] It was impossible with the old nature to be united with God, but in the new nature that we are granted in the water of Baptism because of the resurrection of Christ, we can be united with Him. As St. Paul says in the epistle to the Romans, "Just as Christ was raised from the dead by the glory of the Father, even so we also should walk in newness of life."[99]

The resurrection is the death of the old man. When we are born in the body, we are born carnal, as the Lord said to Nicodemus, "That which is born of the flesh is flesh."[100] The carnal person has a nature that loves the pleasures of the world and the wealth of the world, and

---

98   Galatians 3:27.
99   Romans 6:4.
100 John 3:6.

loves honor, the ego, and pride. Consider, for example, a person who does not have strong faith. You find that they rejoice in money and the pleasures of the world, and rejoice in receiving honor from men. These will neither reach the Kingdom nor understand the mystery of Christ. Therefore, the Lord said to Nicodemus that the person needs to be born again, but this time he is born of the Spirit.

Therefore, the resurrection is the death of the old man, the carnal man, who dies in the water of Baptism. The person who has risen with Christ is living as the new spiritual man, "And those who are Christ's have crucified the flesh with its passions and desires."[101] As St. Paul said, "It is no longer I who live, but Christ lives in me."[102]

6. New Abilities

Through the resurrection of our Lord Jesus Christ, we are granted new abilities, as we read in the second epistle of St. Peter, "As His divine power has given to us all things that pertain to life and godliness, through the knowledge of Him who called us by glory and virtue."[103] So St. Peter is saying that His divine power has given to us all things that we need to live a godly life, which we received through the resurrection of Christ. Therefore, we do not have any excuses.

---

101 Galatians 5:24.
102 Galatians 2:20.
103 2 Peter 1:3.

Because after His death, the Lord bound Satan. And Satan is not unchained as before. There are now restrictions on him. And we are granted the power of the resurrection as St. Paul says, "That I may know Him and the power of His resurrection, and the fellowship of His sufferings."[104]

7. Bearing the Fruit of the Spirit

After His resurrection, Christ ascended to heaven and sent us the Holy Spirit. He had to be risen first before ascending into heaven and entering the Holy place. As we have said, in the fraction of Bright Saturday, "He went within the veil to the Holy place of the Holies, the place into which anyone of human nature cannot enter." And after He entered by His blood, as St. Paul explained in His epistle to the Hebrews,[105] He sent us the Paraclete, the Holy Spirit. And now we are the temple of God, and the Holy Spirit abides in us. Not only are we now granted victory over sin, over Satan, and over temptations, but we can also bear the fruit of the Spirit. Now these virtues can be in our life: "Love, joy, peace, longsuffering, kindness, goodness, faithfulness, gentleness, self-control."[106]

8. New Relationship with the Holy Trinity

Also, through His resurrection, we entered into a new relationship with the Holy Trinity. Before the resurrection,

---

104 Philippians 3:10.
105 See Hebrews 10:19.
106 Galatians 5:22–23.

there was enmity. We were enemies of God. We were not called His people. We were not called His beloved as we read in Hosea.[107] But with the resurrection, the Lord said, "I will call them My people, who were not My people, and her beloved, who was not beloved."[108] We became children of God the Father; we became the bride of the true Bridegroom, our Lord Jesus Christ; and the Holy Spirit abides in us. We enter into this new relationship.

9. Hope

Through the resurrection of Christ, we understand the words we pray in the Litany for the Sick, "The hope of those who have no hope and the help of those who have no helper." We go to the tomb of Christ, and we see that it is empty, which is evidence of the resurrection of Christ. Therefore, we have hope that even if we die, we will be raised again, as we chant in the conclusion of the Creed, "We look for the resurrection of the dead and the life of the age to come. Amen." Now we have this hope, hope in the resurrection, and also hope that we will inherit the kingdom of God, because now we are His children, as St. Paul said in his epistle to the Romans, "We are children of God, and if children, then heirs,"[109] and "The Spirit Himself bears witness with our spirit that we are children of God,"[110] "because you are sons, God has sent forth

---

107　See Hosea 2:23.
108　Romans 9:25.
109　Romans 8:16–17.
110　Romans 8:16.

the Spirit of His Son into your hearts, crying out, 'Abba, Father!'"[111]

10. We Understand the Meaning of Love

Through the resurrection of Christ, we understand what love is: "Greater love has no one than this, than to lay down one's life for his friends."[112] As St. Paul the Apostle says, "God demonstrates His own love toward us, in that while we were still sinners, Christ died for us,"[113] and the love of God the Father, "He who did not spare His own Son, but delivered Him up for us all, how shall He not with Him also freely give us all things?"[114] Now we can reflect on the incomprehensible love of God. That is why St. Paul said, "To know the love of Christ which passes knowledge."[115]

Keep the feast of the Resurrection; come to the aid of Eve who was first to fall, of Her who first embraced the Christ, and made Him known to the disciples. Be a Peter or a John; hasten to the Sepulcher, running together, running against one another, vying in the noble race.

St. Gregory of Nazianzus

Oration XLV XXIV. (NPNF[2] 7)

---

111 Galatians 4:6.
112 John 15:13.
113 Romans 5:8.
114 Romans 8:32.
115 Ephesians 3:19.

7

Meditations on the Resurrection

Why did He Rise on the Third Day?[116]

If Christ had risen before the third day, for example, on the second day or on the same day, the first point to consider is that people would have doubted His death. Some people might have said that He had not actually died but had been in a coma.

The second point is that the body starts to be corrupted after forty-eight hours after death; this is when the process of corruption—the decaying of the body—begins. So if he had risen with the glorious body before the third day, He would not have actually shown us that His body had not seen corruption. But He waited until the third day, when the process of decaying and corruption should have started, and then He rose with the same body, which was not corrupted, as David the prophet said in the psalm, "For You will not leave my soul in Sheol, nor will You

---

116 See St. Athanasius, *On the Incarnation* 26. (NPNF[2] 4).

allow Your Holy One to see corruption."[117] And this is what St. Peter quoted in his sermon in the Book of Acts to show us the glory and power of His body that is united with the divinity, and he said, "He, foreseeing this, spoke concerning the resurrection of the Christ, that His soul was not left in Hades, nor did His flesh see corruption."[118]

But why did He not wait for a longer time than three days, maybe five days or ten days? St. Athanasius said that the disciples were scared. So He did not want them to live in fear for a long time. So three days is a suitable time to prove that His death was real. And by this time, the decaying process would have started, but His body did not decay. If He had waited for a longer time, He would have put His disciples in distress? Therefore, this was a sign of His love and compassion for the disciples.

Also, people were in Jerusalem celebrating the feast of the Passover, and they had not left Jerusalem yet. So the people who had seen His death would hear about His resurrection. But if He had risen ten days or fifteen days after His death, these people would have gone back to their countries and their homes, and they would not have known about His resurrection.

Likewise, if He had risen after a longer time, the people may have thought that He was just a ghost. Nowadays, for example, when any of the saints appears to us, we know that this is the spirit of the saint who appears because their bodies are still here on earth. That is why when the Lord

---

117 Psalms 16:10.

118 Acts 2:31.

rose from the dead, He wanted to emphasize that He rose with His body. It is not just an appearance, like when St. Mary appears right now, or St. George, or any of the saints. He ate and drank with them. He said, "Behold My hands and My feet, that it is I Myself. Handle Me and see, for a spirit does not have flesh and bones as you see I have."[119] Also, "He showed them His hands and His feet."[120] He showed them the marks of the nails and the mark of the spear. Why? To say that He rose with His body. Yes, it is the same body, but in a glorious form.

From Fear to Longing

Before the resurrection, this relationship of human beings with death was full of fear. St. Paul says in his epistle to the Hebrews, "Inasmuch then as the children have partaken of flesh and blood, He Himself likewise shared in the same, that through death He might destroy him who had the power of death, that is, the devil."[121] We, human beings, have flesh and blood. Jesus Christ Himself likewise shared in the same. So, He took full humanity like us. Why? So that by dying on the cross, first, He abolished the power of death, and second, He destroyed Satan, who had the power of death. Third, He might "release those who through fear of death were all their lifetime subject to bondage."[122]

---

119 Luke 24:39.
120 Luke 24:40.
121 Hebrews 2:14.
122 Hebrews 2:15.

Before the resurrection of Christ, all humanity was afraid of death, all of them, because they knew that, after death, everyone went to Hades, even the righteous. That is why everyone was afraid of death, and they were under bondage because of the fear of death. But now, we, the believers in Christ and the believers in the resurrection, are no longer afraid of death. Listen to what St. Paul said about death, "For to me, to live is Christ, and to die is gain."[123]

To any believer, death is gain. They will go to "the place out of which grief, sorrow, and groaning have fled away in the light of Your saints."[124] I will be with God Himself. I will be with all the saints. That is why St. Paul said, "Having a desire to depart and be with Christ, which is far better."[125] That is why we saw the martyrs go to martyrdom, running, not afraid or scared of death. Thousands of people died for the name of Christ.

A big change has happened now in our relationship with death. Not only are we not afraid of death, but we long for it. "I have a desire to depart and be with Christ, which is far better." When St. Paul was in prison, he said, "I know I will be released from prison. But I can be released either this way, meaning to heaven, or that way, to my ministry." So, he said, "I am perplexed. I don't know what to choose. If God asked me to choose, I would say, 'I do not know.' The first choice is far better for me. I have a desire to depart and be with Christ. This is far better. But

---

123 Philippians 1:21.
124 Litany for the Departed.
125 Philippians 1:23.

the second choice, I know I still have obligations toward my children, and I know I need to serve them."[126]

Before Christ, when anyone died—whether Abraham, Isaac, Jacob, or anyone else—Satan took his soul to Hades with him; even John the Baptist, because he died before Christ, before the resurrection, Satan captured his soul. But for us, when we die, the angels will carry our souls, not Satan. Satan has no part in us. Satan has no authority over us.[127] We will not go to Hades, but will go directly to the Paradise of joy, which is far better.

Why was the Resurrection Not Done Publicly?[128]

Why was His crucifixion public, but His resurrection was not public? St. Peter answered this question in the Book of Acts, saying, "Him God raised up on the third day, and showed Him openly, not to all the people, but to witnesses chosen before by God, even to us who ate and drank with Him after He arose from the dead."[129] St. Peter said that His resurrection was not revealed to everyone, but only to some people, chosen by God the Father to be witnesses. St. Peter also mentioned that they ate and drank with Him, so that he may again emphasize that His resurrection is true. He rose with His body after He arose from the dead.

---

126 See Philippians 1:21–26.

127 See Hebrews 2.

128 See St. Athanasius, *On the Incarnation* 32. (NPNF[2] 4).

129 Acts 10:40–41.

St. Athanasius said that one of the attributes of God is that He is invisible, and we know God by His works and by His deeds. That is exactly what St. Paul said in the epistle to the Romans, "For since the creation of the world His invisible attributes are clearly seen, being understood by the things that are made, even His eternal power and Godhead, so that they are without excuse."[130] God is invisible, but we know Him by His works, by what He made in the creation. We can know His eternal power and His Godhead. So those who deny the existence of God have no excuse. St. Athanasius said that God is invisible, and this is His attribute. That is why He did not appear to all, but appeared only to some people whom God chose and appointed to be witnesses of His resurrection.

Before the crucifixion, He was living with us as a human being, fully human and fully God. But after resurrection, He became invisible, except to these witnesses, and then ascended to heaven. And one time, as St. Paul said, "He was seen by over five hundred brethren at once, of whom the greater part remain to the present."[131] So these 500 people definitely did not see an illusion. If they saw Christ, then it is a fact that they truly saw Him. And if St. Paul were making this story up, most of them were alive, and they would have challenged him.

And do you think that I would make up a story, and at the end, I would shed my blood and die for a fake

---

130 Romans 1:20.
131 1 Corinthians 15:6.

story that I made up? The Apostles died mainly because they preached the resurrection of Christ. St. Paul died because he was preaching the resurrection of Christ. So, why would I make up a story, and at the end, I die for it, knowing it is a lie?

So God chose witnesses, people who were true witnesses. In the story of Lazarus the poor, Abraham said to the rich man, "If they do not hear Moses and the prophets, neither will they be persuaded though one rise from the dead."[132] So even if Jesus appeared publicly for everybody, some people would doubt Him. Also, when Jesus raised Lazarus from the dead, we read in the Gospel of St. John that the Jews wanted to kill Lazarus, as though Jesus could not raise him again if they killed him. Nowadays, for example, St. Mary appeared in Egypt over fifty years ago, but some people, until now, do not believe it, and they doubt this. People who refuse to believe will continue to refuse to believe. That is why God did not entrust everyone with the good news of the resurrection, only faithful witnesses whom God appointed to be witnesses of His resurrection, as St. Peter said.

---

132 Luke 16:31.

But even if, without any disease and without any pain, He had hidden His body away privately and by Himself "in a corner," or in a desert place, or in a house, or anywhere, and afterwards suddenly appeared and said that He had been raised from the dead, He would have seemed on all hands to be telling idle tales, and what He said about the Resurrection would have been all the more discredited, as there was no one at all to witness to His death. Now, death must precede resurrection, as it would be no resurrection did not death precede; so that if the death of His body had taken place anywhere in secret, the death not being apparent nor taking place before witnesses, His Resurrection too had been hidden and without evidence.

St. Athanasius the Apostolic

On the Incarnation 23. (NPNF[2] 4)

8

What is the Evidence of the Resurrection of Christ?

1. The Death of Christ Testifies to the Resurrection

We read in the Gospel of St. Mark that when Pilate was told that Christ was already dead, he marveled,[133] because a person takes a long time to die on the wood of the cross. And they were forced sometimes to break their legs, so that there would no longer be support for them to breathe, and so they would die by suffocation because they cannot draw their breath as a result of the body being pulled down. This led Pilate to confirm with the centurion, seeking to verify the death of Christ. So how does the death of Christ indicate His resurrection?

---

133 See Mark 15:44.

The Lord Jesus Christ made a very important statement: "I have power to lay it down, and I have power to take it again,"[134] speaking about His life. The time of death comes to all of us, and when it comes, that is it. The person does not have control over the time of death. When a person's life ends, he dies. The situation, however, is different with respect to Christ. He surrendered Himself to death by His will and power alone.

When He said, "I have power to lay it down," this means He Himself surrendered His spirit in the hand of the Father, as He said, "Father, 'into Your hands I commit My spirit,'"[135] at the minute, second, and moment that Christ had determined before the foundation of the world. Therefore, when we speak about the death of the Lord Jesus Christ, the sound theological expression is as that used in the Divine Liturgy of St. Cyril, which says, "The death, which He accepted by His own will for us all."[136] That is, He permitted death to approach Him. He has power to lay it down and power to take it again— "You gave Yourself up of Your own will and authority alone."[137]

The devil used to receive the people's souls before the resurrection; for this reason, He said, "The ruler of this world is coming, and he has nothing in Me."[138] The devil could not receive His spirit, because He is the Son

---

134 John 10:18.
135 Luke 23:46.
136 The Liturgy of St. Cyril – The Institution Narrative.
137 The Liturgy of St. Gregory – The Institution Narrative.
138 John 14:30.

of God. He said, "I have power to lay it down, and I have power to take it again,"[139] and He said to Pilate, "You could have no power at all against Me unless it had been given you from above."[140] Therefore, His own death in itself confirms His resurrection.

2. The Empty Tomb

The chief priests and Pharisees were afraid that the disciples might steal the body of Christ and say that He had risen from the dead. For this reason, they put a large stone on the [door of the] tomb, sealed it, and assigned a guard to keep watch. It was not easy for the disciples to come, for example, then remove the seal, and take away the stone, without being caught by the guard. This is impossible. The empty tomb in itself is proof of the resurrection of the Lord Jesus Christ. The tomb of Christ is present until today, and many of us have visited it. And the light that appears on the eve of the Feast of the Resurrection is also a powerful proof for the resurrection of Christ—glory be to Him. When St. Peter and St. John went and found it empty, and Mary Magdalene found angels in it, all these are proofs of the resurrection of Christ.

3. The Linen Cloths

The Jews asked the guard to say that the disciples came and stole Him while they were asleep. First of all, if this

---

139 John 10:18.
140 John 19:11.

allegation of sleeping had been true, they would have been punished for it, so why were they not punished for it? Why were the disciples not punished, though they were in Jerusalem, and it was easy for them to seize them, since they broke Pilate's seal?

But concerning the linen cloths, St. John says, "[Peter] saw the linen cloths lying there, and the handkerchief that had been around His head, not lying with the linen cloths, but folded together in a place by itself."[141] If someone were to steal, would he steal the body, but put the linen cloths in one place, and fold the handkerchief and put it somewhere else? This is impossible, of course, because the thief would steal and run away quickly, and then he would hide.

Studies were done on the shroud that is currently located in Turin, Italy. You can read the books that were published about the shroud, and watch the videos that were done about it. By only studying the shroud, all the sufferings and torments Christ went through were proven, and the resurrection was proven too. Some of these researchers who were studying the shroud were atheists, and their aim was to prove that this was not the shroud of Christ and that Christians were lying to people, saying that this piece of cloth was the shroud of Christ. But when these researchers began studying the shroud of Christ, they ended up believing in Christ and in His marvelous resurrection, after being atheists.

---

141 John 20:6–7.

4. The Seal

It is said that the seal used to be put in place in the presence of the Roman guard assigned to guard the Roman emblem that represented the power and authority of Rome. That is to say, they used to bring the soldiers, put the seal in front of them, and say to them, "This represents the power of Rome. If you allow anyone to break the seal, then you will be sentenced to death." These were the laws of Rome. Therefore, it was not possible to open the door without breaking the seal. And breaking the seal was considered a heinous crime against the Roman Empire.

But how was it broken? "An angel of the Lord descended from heaven, and came and rolled back the stone from the door,"[142] and so the seal was broken. But who would they put on trial here? When the guard saw the angel, the Scripture says, "And the guards shook for fear of him, and became like dead men."[143] The Lord Jesus Christ rose before the stone was rolled back. Archangel Michael rolled the stone back to announce the resurrection of Christ to the women who were coming to the tomb on Sunday morning to put the spices on the body of Christ.

5. The Guard

If someone studies the Roman guard, they will discover that they were fully equipped. There used to be two

---

142   Matthew 28:2.
143   Matthew 28:4.

groups of four men specially trained for guarding. They were very well trained and at the ready for any danger. If the disciples had approached these to steal the body, they would have killed them right there and then. Therefore, it is not possible for the soldiers to say that they were sleeping, because the punishment for sleeping while on guard is death. Their saying that they were sleeping, and nothing happened to them, is proof that this was a conspiracy. Therefore, Christ rose, and the guards were not sleeping, but from the appearance of an angel and the earthquake, they were like dead men, as we read in the Scripture:

> And behold, there was a great earthquake; for an angel of the Lord descended from heaven, and came and rolled back the stone from the door, and sat on it. His countenance was like lightning, and his clothing as white as snow. And the guards shook for fear of him, and became like dead men.[144]

6. Suffering and Martyrdom of the Disciples

All the Apostles, except St. John, were martyred. Even St. John was tortured and exiled to the island of Patmos. What would make the Apostles, who supposedly stole the body of Christ, who then fabricated a story about His resurrection, and who fabricated another story about

---

144 Matthew 28:2–4.

His ascension, accept to die for the sake of a story they knew they had themselves fabricated? Who, in their right mind, would do such a thing?

Consider terrorism, for example. Those who plan know that what they are saying is wrong; therefore, they do not risk their lives, but rather they brainwash young men and make them execute the terroristic plans. Those who execute are the ones deceived, while the leaders, those who plan, do not believe in a religion, nor do they do these for religious reasons. The reasons are rather political, and they seek power.

Let us apply this to the Apostles. All of them were martyred. If they had been the ones planning, they would have deceived other people and let them be martyred, while they would not themselves have been martyred. Apart from martyrdom, they were tortured. St. Peter, for example, was scourged, along with the rest of the Apostles; but St. Peter said, "We ought to obey God rather than men."[145] The Scripture then says, "So they departed from the presence of the council, rejoicing that they were counted worthy to suffer shame for His name."[146]

Who would make a story up, and then die for it, knowing that it is a lie? Not just one of the Apostles did this, but eleven of them (including St. Matthias), apart from St. John. Who can endure the tortures? St. Paul said, "Concerning the resurrection of the dead I am being

---

145 Acts 5:29.
146 Acts 5:41.

judged."[147] This means that all the suffering St. Paul went through, ending in his martyrdom, was because of the resurrection of the dead.

7. The Appearances of the Lord Jesus Christ

Our Lord Jesus Christ appeared many times, but I would like to speak about one of these appearances. In his first epistle to the Corinthians, St. Paul the Apostle says, "He was seen by over five hundred brethren at once, of whom the greater part remain to the present."[148] This means that 500 people were assembled, and at the time of St. Paul's writing his epistle, most of these were still alive. Is it reasonable to think that these 500 imagined that there was an appearance and that they saw Christ, while He did not appear to them? Not reasonable.

Concluding Remarks

All these are powerful proofs of the resurrection of Christ. The Church was founded upon the resurrection of Christ, and the martyrs shed their blood for this matter: the matter that Christ rose from the dead. Therefore, the Lord cared very much that the Apostles, who would preach the resurrection, were themselves completely certain about His resurrection. And when He found that one of the Apostles had a doubt, who was Thomas, He appeared to him especially and said to him, "Reach your

---

147 Acts 24:21.
148 1 Corinthians 15:6.

finger here, and look at My hands; and reach your hand here, and put it into My side. Do not be unbelieving, but believing."[149] And it is said that when Thomas tried to touch Christ, he felt an awesome power coming out of the body of the Lord, making him cry out, confess, and say, "My Lord and my God!"[150] And so, the Lord chastised him and said, "Thomas, because you have seen Me, you have believed. Blessed are those who have not seen and yet have believed."[151]

Nowadays, many people doubt the resurrection of Christ, doubt the existence of God, doubt the stories of the Holy Scripture, and doubt many things. They may say, "Are there mistakes in the Holy Scripture or not?" Sowing doubt is everywhere, but we, as children of God, need to have a strong faith. For this reason, the Gospel of St. John concludes with a very important saying: "And truly Jesus did many other signs in the presence of His disciples, which are not written in this book; but these are written that you may believe that Jesus is the Christ, the Son of God."[152] St. John did not make a record of all the miracles that the Lord Jesus Christ performed, but rather recorded some miracles and some events.

The goal of the writing of the Gospel of St. John—and the New Testament—is that people may believe in Christ; and not only believing in Christ, but also believing in His resurrection, as St. Paul the Apostle

---

149 John 20:27.
150 John 20:28.
151 John 20:29.
152 John 20:30–31.

said, "And if Christ is not risen, then our preaching is empty and your faith is also empty.... And if Christ is not risen, your faith is futile; you are still in your sins!"[153] Therefore, believing in the truth of the resurrection is very important, "that believing you may have life in His name."[154] Believing in the resurrection is a condition for receiving eternal life.

I wish that You would vouchsafe to come to this sepulcher of mine, O Lord Jesus, that You would wash me with Your tears, since in my hardened eyes I possess not such tears as to be able to wash away my offence. If You shall weep for me I shall be saved; if I am worthy of Your tears I shall cleanse the stench of all my offences; if I am worthy that You weep but a little, You will call me out of the tomb of this body and will say: "Come forth," that my meditations may not be kept confined in the narrow limits of this body, but may go forth to Christ, and move in the light, that I may think no more on works of darkness but on works of light. For he who thinks on sins endeavors to shut himself up within his own consciousness.

St. Ambrose of Milan

On Repentance II.VIII.71. (NPNF² 10)

---

153 1 Corinthians 15:14, 17.
154 John 20:31.